# EARTHQUAKES

## BY
## NEIL MORRIS

# WHAT IS AN EARTHQUAKE?

**ARISTOTLE**

Aristotle (384-322 BC),
the great Greek philosopher
and scientist, believed that
the Earth had grown like a
living thing to its present size.
He also thought that our rocky planet
was honeycombed with underground
caves that sucked up the world's winds.
When fires inside the Earth heated the
winds beyond a certain point, they
exploded. These explosions, Aristotle
thought, caused earthquakes. It was
thousands of years before scientists
began to discover the real cause
of earthquakes.

**A**n earthquake is a shaking of the ground caused by movements beneath the Earth's surface. Strong earthquakes can collapse buildings, bridges and other structures, causing great damage and loss of life. The Earth's surface is made up of an outer layer of rocks, called its crust. The crust is cracked into huge pieces that fit together like a giant jigsaw puzzle. These pieces, called plates, slowly move and rub against each other, squeezing and stretching the rocks and causing an enormous build-up of pressure. When the pressure becomes very great, underground rocks break and shift. This release of pressure sends out the shock waves that produce an earthquake and make the ground tremble at the surface. There are around 11 million earthquakes each year worldwide, of which about 34,000 are strong enough to be felt.

CRUST
MANTLE
OUTER CORE
INNER CORE

**BENEATH THE SURFACE**

**Beneath the Earth's crust is a soft mantle, made up of hot, partially molten rock.** The Earth's core is made up of iron and nickel, and is solid at the centre. The crust can be up to 70 km (43 miles) thick beneath the world's biggest mountain ranges. Most earthquakes begin in the crust not far below ground, but sometimes they can occur up to 700 km (435 miles) beneath the Earth's surface.

**ANDES MOUNTAINS**

The Andes is the longest mountain range in the world, stretching down the whole of South America for 7,200 km (4,474 miles). The mountains were created by the collision of the Nazca Oceanic Plate with the South American Continental Plate. In 1970, an earthquake off the Peruvian coast caused a landslide on a high Andean peak, and more than 66,000 people were killed.

## ROCK STRATA

**The rocks that make up the Earth's plates are themselves made of layers, called strata.** As the plates move, the strata are pushed, pulled, bent and folded. The forces beneath the Earth are immense, but movement at the surface is very slight and folding may take thousands of years. If the strata are bent so much that they break, they form a crack called a fault.

*Curving strata are very clearly shown in this photograph of a dry river valley in Namibia.*

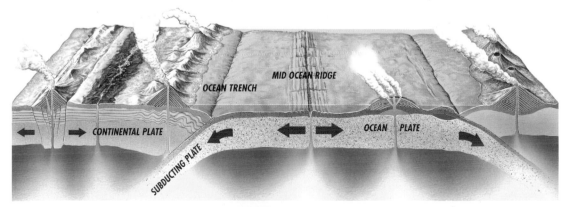

## PLUNGING PLATES

**Some of the world's biggest earthquakes occur in regions where one of the crust's plates is forced beneath another plate as the two collide in a process called subduction.** This is usually an oceanic plate, covered by sea, running into a thicker continental plate, covered by land. The plunging ocean plate grinds against the upper plate, melting parts of both and creating volcanoes and earthquakes.

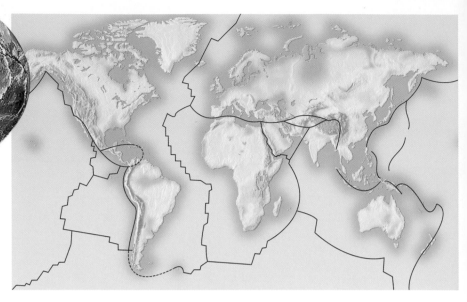

*This satellite picture shows the 'Ring of Fire'. The sites of major earthquakes are marked red, and plate boundaries are shown in yellow.*

## THE WORLD'S PLATES

**The plates that make up the Earth's crust are constantly moving, by just a few centimetres each year.** This small movement sets off earthquakes and volcanoes, as well as creating mountain ranges and deep-sea trenches. The lines on the map show the edges of plates, where most earthquakes occur.

## MID-ATLANTIC RIDGE

**São Miguel is the largest of the islands that make up the Azores.**
This group of volcanic islands lies in the North Atlantic Ocean, about 1,300 km (808 miles) west of Portugal. They lie on the slopes of the Mid-Atlantic Ridge, an underwater range of mountains formed by molten rock as the American Plate moves apart from the Eurasian and African Plates. The islands are frequently shaken by earthquakes.

# ALL OVER THE WORLD

About 150 years ago, an Irish engineer named Robert Mallet started collecting information about the exact location of earthquakes around the Mediterranean Sea. He plotted almost 7,000 earthquakes on a map and discovered a pattern, but he had no idea why this should be. We now know that about three-quarters of the world's earthquakes occur in a zone around the Pacific Ocean called the 'Ring of Fire', so-called because it is dotted with active volcanoes. Another earthquake belt runs across southern Europe and Asia, from the Mediterranean through the Middle East and the Himalayas to Indonesia. The two great earthquake belts meet near the island of New Guinea. Both are situated along the edges of plates.

**NEW ZEALAND**

**The eruption of Mount Ruapehu in 1996 may have been caused by an earthquake.** The Pacific and Indo-Australian Plates meet beneath the islands of New Zealand. This collision causes many earthquakes and volcanoes. New Zealand has about 400 earthquakes every year, but only about 100 of them are strong enough to be felt.

**CHINA**

**In 1556, an earthquake killed the almost unbelievable number of 830,000 people in central China.** In 1976, at least 240,000 were killed by an earthquake in the northeast of the country. Today, China has many cities with more than a million inhabitants. When large numbers of people live close together in or near tall buildings, the human risks from earthquakes are very high.

**EUROPE**

**In 1997, a series of tremors in central Italy caused part of the Basilica of St Francis in Assisi to collapse.** Falling masonry killed four people, including two Franciscan friars, and many frescoes by the famous painter Giotto were destroyed. The frescoes are being carefully pieced together and restored.

**THE UNITED STATES**

**Reelfoot Lake, in Tennessee, was created by earthquakes in the 19th century.** In 1811 and 1812, earthquakes in the southern USA were so strong that they caused the Mississippi River to flow backwards for half an hour. River water poured into low-lying forests and created new lakes. Some still exist today. It is said that the quakes were so strong that they shook and rang church bells in Boston, 1,700 km (1,056 miles) away.

# CRACKING FAULTS
..................

**A**s the plates that make up the Earth's crust move and jostle together, they put rocks under such great strain that they sometimes crack. The places where the rocks crack are called faults, and the lines the cracks create are known as fault lines. Large fault lines may go deep into underground rocks and stretch along whole continents. The world's biggest fault lines, like the strongest earthquakes, are found near the edges of plates. Some large faults split open the ground when they move, and others push areas of land up or cause it to sink. After an earthquake, when energy has been released, the rock masses on either side of the fault are locked together in new positions. The stresses and strains that caused the original earthquake often begin again and go on building up, until eventually they cause another quake.

*Clear evidence of a horizontal fault can be seen from the road marking in this photograph (near Landers, California, in 1992). Earthquakes along horizontal faults have a devastating effect on buildings and other structures, and they are common in California, China and Turkey.*

*On the island of Iceland, a large open crack marks the spot where the eastern edge of the North American Plate (on the left in the photograph) meets the western edge of the Eurasian Plate (on the right). The two plates are moving apart at a rate of about 2.5 cm (1 inch) a year, at the same time widening the Atlantic Ocean by the same amount.*

## GREAT RIFT VALLEY

**All the way from the Red Sea to Mozambique, an immense system of faults cuts deep across the face of East Africa.** In parts, the Great Rift Valley is up to 100 km (62 miles) wide. It has some of Africa's most spectacular scenery, including lakes and volcanoes. Movements of the African and Somali Plates have formed most parts of the valley, pulling apart the land. In Kenya, this has been going on for millions of years.

NORMAL
FAULT

REVERSE
FAULT

HORIZONTAL FAULT

## DIFFERENT FAULTS

There are different types of faults, depending on the movement of the rocks, and they fall into three main groups. A 'normal' fault is caused when tension in the Earth's crust pulls two blocks of rock apart, so that one block slips down along the fault plane.
When the tension pushes two blocks of rock together, one of the blocks is forced to move up the fault plane and form a 'reverse' fault.
'Horizontal' faults form when blocks of rock slide past each other sideways.

## NORTHRIDGE, 1994

**At 4.30 on the morning of 17 January 1994, an earthquake shook the town of Northridge, 30 km (19 miles) north of Los Angeles.** The shaking, which lasted up to 20 seconds, knocked out 10 road bridges and closed three major highways. Sixty people were killed and 25,000 were left homeless. Northridge lies on a small fault running from the San Andreas to the ocean.

# SAN ANDREAS FAULT

**O**ne of the world's most famous geological features, the San Andreas Fault, cuts along the Pacific coast of **California, USA.** This horizontal fault is 1,200 km (746 miles) long, forming part of the boundary between the Pacific and North American Plates. The two plates constantly slide past each other, at a rate of about 5 cm (2 inches) a year. Many smaller fault lines criss-cross the region, some connecting up with the San Andreas. This is one of the world's major earthquake zones, with over 20,000 tremors recorded every year.

*Californian schoolchildren are used to earthquake drills as the constant threat of earthquakes is part of their daily life and school routine.*

## SAN FRANCISCO, 1906

**A huge earthquake shook San Francisco at 5.12 on the morning of 18 April 1906.** The city shook for up to a minute as the San Andreas Fault slipped up to 6 metres (20 ft) along 430 km (267 miles) of its length. About 28,000 buildings were destroyed, with entire streets collapsing. Out of a population of 400,000, at least 3,000 people were killed and 225,000 were left homeless.

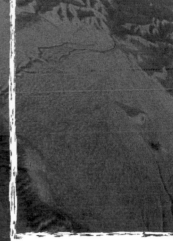

The San Andreas Fault can be clearly seen from the air, like a deep scar across the landscape. Scientists think that the two ends of the San Andreas Fault are perhaps most dangerous: Cape Mendocino, north of San Francisco, and Imperial Valley, south of Los Angeles.

SAN ANDREAS FAULT

San Francisco

Los Angeles

NORTH AMERICA

This map shows how the San Andreas Fault runs the length of the Californian coast. The Pacific Ocean and the strip of land west of the Fault lie on the Pacific Plate, which is sliding northwestwards. The rest of the land is moving very slowly towards the south-east. Los Angeles, with a population of 14.5 million, is very close to the fault, and San Francisco sits practically on top of it.

## SAN FRANCISCO, 1906
### A SAN FRANCISCO JOURNALIST

The bureau at the back of the room came towards me. It was springing up and down and from side to side. It danced...in a zigzag course...it was almost funny. Now I turned on my sense of hearing. I heard the crash of falling buildings, the rumble of avalanches of bricks, the groans of tortured girders.

### THE NEXT DAY

After darkness, thousands of the homeless were making their way with their blankets and scant provisions to Golden Gate Park and the beach to find shelter. Everybody is prepared to leave the city, for the belief is firm that San Francisco will be totally destroyed. Downtown everything is ruin.

## FRISCO ON FIRE

In 1906, most San Francisco buildings that withstood the shaking of the earthquake did not survive the fires. Many of these were caused by overturned stoves. Water pipes were burst by the earthquake on the outskirts of the city, leaving San Franciscans with little or no water to put the flames out. The fires raged on for three days, as survivors tried to find safe areas outside the city.

## ALASKA, 1964

**On 27 March 1964, an earthquake hit the town of Anchorage, in Alaska, starting a landslide and killing 131 people.** Houses that had been built on loose rock and soil were carried a long way by the landslide, some as far as 600 metres (1,968 ft). The epicentre of the earthquake was discovered to be 130 km (81 miles) away from Anchorage, and the focus was 20 km (12 miles) beneath the surface. The quake also caused a tsunami (see pages 16/17), which hit the coast of Alaska with waves more than 5 metres (16 ft) high and reached as far south as California.

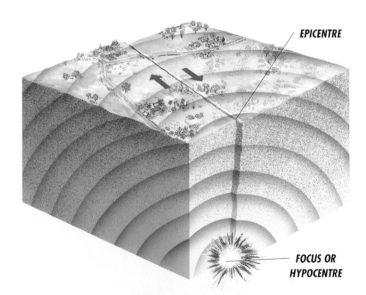

*EPICENTRE*

*FOCUS OR HYPOCENTRE*

## FOCUS AND EPICENTRE

**The focus of an earthquake is deep underground, at the exact point on a fault where the rocks first crack and move.** The epicentre is the point on the surface of the Earth directly above the focus. Often the pattern of seismic waves is not as neat as it appears here: waves can be bent as they pass from one type of rock to another, and body waves can be reflected back down into the ground when they reach the surface.

# SEISMIC WAVES

**T**he exact underground spot where rocks jolt and cause an earthquake is called the focus, or hypocentre. This spot may be hundreds of kilometres under the ground or beneath the sea. The movement of the rocks causes vibrations, called seismic waves, to move out in every direction from the focus. The seismic waves move very fast, and we feel them when they reach the surface. They are at their strongest at the point on the Earth's surface directly above the focus. As the waves spread out from the focus, they get weaker. The general amount of damage caused by an earthquake's seismic waves depends to some extent on the kind of rocks that make up the vibrating surface. Solid granite and massive layers of sandstone, for example, shake much less than the sandy soil that is often found near rivers and coasts. When rocks begin to crack along a fault, they sometimes send out a gentle tremor or series of tremors before the main earthquake. These tremors are called foreshocks, and they provide a warning for people in the region to seek a safe place.

## LONG-DISTANCE DAMAGE

One evening in 1989, at 5.04 p.m., the ground in San Francisco, USA, shook violently for 15 seconds. More than 28,000 houses were damaged, 63 people were killed, and nearly 4,000 were injured. Scientists later worked out that the epicentre of the earthquake was 120 km (75 miles) south of San Francisco, in the Santa Cruz mountains.

## BODY WAVES

*The vibrations that travel deep underground from the focus of an earthquake are called body waves. There are two kinds: primary or P waves, and secondary or S waves. P waves travel faster, at about 21,600 km/h (13,422 mph) – many times the speed of sound! They push and pull on the rocks, with an effect like a shunting train. S waves shake rocks up and down and from side to side in a snakelike movement.*

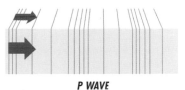

*P WAVE*

*S WAVE*

## SURFACE WAVES

*At the surface, there are also two kinds of seismic waves, named after the scientists who first described them. Rayleigh waves move up and down, while Love waves push the rocks from side to side as they travel forwards. Surface waves are slower than body waves, but they cause most damage to structures on the surface, partly because they take longer to pass through.*

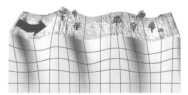

*RAYLEIGH WAVE*

*LOVE WAVE*

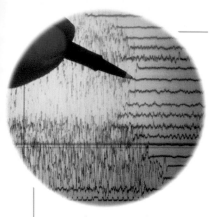

A modern seismograph traces ground movements onto paper wrapped around a rotating drum. The resulting wavy lines on a graph make up a seismogram (above), which can be printed out or shown on a computer screen. The bigger the earthquake, the greater the ground movement and the higher the peaks traced on a seismogram.

## CHILE, 1960

**To measure the largest earthquakes, seismologists also use the moment magnitude scale.** This is based on readings for the size of the fault's rupture, the amount of movement at the surface, and the duration of the earthquake. The resulting figure is about the same as the Richter scale for earthquakes up to magnitude 7. The highest recorded moment magnitude was 9.5, for an earthquake on the coast of Chile in 1960, which also caused a volcano to erupt and killed 5,700 people. The Richter magnitude of this quake was 8.3.

## THE RICHTER SCALE

*The American seismologist Charles F. Richter (1900-85) developed his numbering system in 1935. Each number on the Richter scale represents a 10-times increase in the ground movement recorded on a seismograph. So in an earthquake of magnitude 7, the ground moves 100 times as much as in a quake of magnitude 5.*

| MAGNITUDE | DESCRIPTION | AVERAGE PER YEAR |
|-----------|-------------|------------------|
| 0-1.9 | - | 700,000 |
| 2-2.9 | - | 300,000 |
| 3-3.9 | MINOR | 40,000 |
| 4-4.9 | LIGHT | 6,200 |
| 5-5.9 | MODERATE | 800 |
| 6-6.9 | STRONG | 120 |
| 7-7.9 | MAJOR | 18 |
| 8-8.9 | GREAT | 1 IN 10-20 YEARS |

# MEASUREMENT

**T**he scientists who specialize in studying earthquakes are called seismologists. They use measuring instruments called seismographs, or seismometers, to record the pattern of seismic waves and work out the strength and duration of each earthquake. Readings are taken at several different points so that the exact location of the quake's focus and epicentre can be pinpointed. The strength of a quake's movement, based on its effects and damage, is shown as a number on a scale. The first scale was invented by an Italian, Guiseppe Mercalli, in 1902. Today, the best-known classification of earthquakes is the Richter scale, which uses measurements from seismographs to describe and compare the strength and size of earthquakes.

## MILNE'S SEISMOGRAPH

British engineer and seismologist John Milne (1850-1913) became Professor of Geology at the University of Tokyo, and on his first day in Japan was greeted by an earthquake. Milne set to work devising his own seismograph, which recorded the movement of a pendulum, first on revolving smoked paper and later on photographic film. Milne collected the results of more than 8,000 earthquakes in Japan alone. He formed a Seismological Society in 1880, the first such organization anywhere in the world.

## INTENSITY NEAR EPICENTRE

| |
| --- |
| *RECORDED BUT NOT FELT* |
| *RECORDED BUT NOT FELT* |
| *FELT BY SOME* |
| *FELT BY MANY* |
| *SLIGHT DAMAGE* |
| *DAMAGING* |
| *DESTRUCTIVE* |
| *DEVASTATING* |

*This instrument was invented around AD 130 by a Chinese astronomer and mathematician named Chang Heng (AD 78-139). Inside the pot was a pendulum, which would be made to swing by any Earth tremors. The swinging pendulum would knock a bronze ball from one of the dragon's mouths. The ball dropped into a toad's mouth. The position of this toad showed the direction from which the tremor was coming. It is said that in AD 138 the seismograph allowed Chang Heng to announce a major earthquake 600 km (373 miles) away, long before news of its damage arrived by messengers on horseback.*

# LISBON, 1755

**O**n the morning of 1 November 1755, many of Lisbon's 275,000 citizens were in church, lighting candles for All Saints' Day. At 9.40, worshippers in the Portuguese city's central cathedral suddenly heard a terrible rumbling noise. The cathedral shook, and people ran out into the streets in time to see the ground heaving. Buildings throughout the city instantly collapsed and killed thousands of people. Many survivors ran to the harbour, but were then horrified to see huge waves approaching along the Tagus River from the Atlantic Ocean. The first of these smashed over the harbour at 11.00. There was even worse to come. Within a few hours, overturned stoves and lamps started fires that were whipped up by whirling winds. A huge fire swept through the city and burned all the wooden remains and many of the dead bodies. This terrible earthquake, with the resultant flooding and fires, killed around 60,000 people.

### MODERN LISBON

**Lisbon was quickly rebuilt after the earthquake and today has a population of 1.8 million, and is a popular city with tourists.** The oldest part of the city has steep, narrow streets, but in the newer districts, there are straight, wide streets and spacious squares. The docks stretch along the waterfront for 10 km (6 miles). In 1966 a long suspension bridge was built across the Tagus River.

## LISBON, 1755
### FROM VOLTAIRE'S CANDIDE (1759)

*They felt the earth tremble beneath them. The sea boiled up in the harbour and smashed the vessels lying at anchor. Whirlwinds of flame and ashes covered the streets and squares, houses collapsed, roofs were thrown into foundations and the foundations crumbled ... 'This earthquake is nothing new,' replied Pangloss. 'The town of Lima in America felt the same shocks last year. Same causes, same effects; there is surely a vein of sulphur running underground from Lima to Lisbon.'*

### CITY IN RUINS

**About three-quarters of all Lisbon's buildings were destroyed.** Records show that all of the city's 40 parish churches were damaged, and half were completely ruined. Fires burned throughout the city for days. Priceless paintings by masters such as Titian, Rubens and Correggio were burned to ashes. Most survivors left Lisbon, and many set up camp in the hills.

# LISABONA

This engraving shows waves overwhelming ships in the harbour. Some buildings have been swept out to sea, and fires are raging. It is thought that one of the huge sea waves was as high as 12 metres (39 ft). Seismologists have estimated that the Lisbon earthquake might have been as strong as 8.7 on the Richter scale. They believe the epicentre was on the bed of the Atlantic Ocean, perhaps near the edge of the Eurasian and African Plates. It is also said that church bells had begun to peal thousands of kilometres away, waves appeared on the surface of Loch Ness in Scotland, and canal boats in Amsterdam were ripped from their moorings.

## KANT

The German philosopher Immanuel Kant (1724-1804) reported that eight days before the earthquake, the ground near Cadiz, a Spanish port around the coast from Lisbon, was covered with worms that had suddenly crawled out of the soil. This was not the first report of strange behaviour by animals before earthquakes and other disasters, and it was of great interest to scientists.

A General View of the CITY of LISBON the Capital of the Kingdom of Portugal before the late dreadful Earthquake on Nov.r 1.st 1755.

*This painting shows how the port of Lisbon looked before the great earthquake. It became the capital of Portugal in 1256 and quickly became one of Europe's leading cities. It was the chief port serving the vast Portuguese Empire.*

# TSUMAMIS

**S**eaquakes – earthquakes that occur beneath the ocean floor – can create huge waves that sweep across the sea. These waves are called tsunamis, from the Japanese for 'harbour waves'. They got their name because they are particularly destructive when they reach harbours, or any coastline. They are also called seismic sea waves, and sometimes tidal waves, but this is misleading because they have nothing to do with tides. Tsunamis are caused by the seismic waves sent out by seaquakes, which shake the ocean floor and then the water above. In the open ocean, a tsunami moves very fast, sometimes up to 1,000 km/h (621 mph). Out in the deep, the speeding wave may be just 30 cm (12 inches) high. But as the wave reaches shallower water near the coast, it slows down and at the same time builds up to its greatest height, which may be up to 30 metres (98 ft).

## EASTER ISLAND

**The great Chilean earthquake of 1960 caused three tsunamis that crossed the Pacific Ocean.** On their way they hit the small volcanic Easter Island, which is almost 3,800 km (2,361 miles) from the South American coast. The tsunami knocked over some of the mysterious ancient stone statues for which the island is famous.

## NICARAGUA, 1992

*On the evening of 1 September 1992, two men were sitting in their boat in the harbour of the Nicaraguan port of San Juan del Sur. Darkness fell. Suddenly they heard a thump as their boat struck the harbour floor – at a point which was normally more than 6 metres (20 ft) deep. The two men struggled to keep their boat from capsizing, and then looked towards the port. They could see the lights of the town through the crest of the wave that had just passed beneath their boat. Then the lights went out. The port had been hit by a tsunami.*

### DAMAGE AT SEA

*This boat was grounded by a tsunami that hit the island of Kodiak, off the coast of Alaska, USA. Tsunamis are very dangerous to shipping, especially if a vessel is close to the coast.*

This artist's impression shows what it is like when a tsunami hits the shores of Southeast Asia. The mountain in the background shows the great link between volcanoes, earthquakes and tsunamis as any shaking of the sea bed can trigger giant waves. The buildings in the foreground will be swept away by the tremendous force of the water. A tsunami which hit Japan in 1771 was reported as reaching a height of 85 metres (279 ft).

## NICARAGUA, 1992

**On 1 September 1992, a seaquake measuring 7 on the Richter scale shook the Pacific Ocean floor, 100 km (62 miles) off the Nicaraguan coast in Central America.** Many Nicaraguans did not even feel the ground tremble, but soon a 300 km (186 miles) stretch of coastline was hit by tsunamis as high as 10 metres (33 ft). The waves killed 170 people and left more than 13,000 homeless.

## HOW IT FORMS

An earthquake shakes the sea bed, which in turn shakes the water above it. This sets off a tsunami, which builds up as it nears the shore. About three-quarters of damaging tsunamis occur in the Pacific, so Hawaii is the ideal location for the Pacific Tsunami Warning Centre. Advance warnings give people time to evacuate coastal regions.

## REFUGEE CAMP

**When people's homes are destroyed by earthquakes or landslides, they need temporary shelter until they can start to rebuild their lives.** Tents and other makeshift homes are also safer after major earthquakes, in case of aftershocks.

## INDIA, 1993
### BURIED FOR FIVE DAYS

*Early on the morning of 30 September 1993, a large earthquake hit the Indian state of Maharashtra, killing more than 12,000 people. Seventeen villages were completely destroyed and a further 119 villages were badly damaged. In the village of Magrul, an 18-month-old baby named Priya was trapped beneath the rubble. Five days later, she still had not been found and her mother, who was in hospital with severe injuries, had almost given up hope.*

*Then, as rescuers still went on digging, baby Priya was found, alive and well.*

*The only worry for the rescuers was that the child would not accept a drink from anybody. They sent for her grandmother, and when she gave her water, the child drank. It was just that Priya would not accept anything from strangers. Today, the little girl says that she wants to be a*

## KAZAKHSTAN

**Alma-Ata, the largest city in Kazakhstan in central Asia, has a population of more than a million.** The city is in a valley in the foothills of the Tien Shan mountain range, and the region is very prone to landslides. Alma-Ata itself was virtually destroyed by earthquakes in 1887 and 1911, and in 1921 a mudflow caused great damage. In an effort to stop this happening again, engineers used an explosion to deliberately set off a landslide in 1966. The slide blocked up a gorge, and when another natural mudflow occurred in 1973, its effects on local people were greatly reduced.

## LOOKING FOR SURVIVORS

**In 1970, the Peruvian town of Yungay completely disappeared beneath the landslide, and 66,000 people were killed.** Landslides are such a common event in the Andes mountains that the International Union for Geological Sciences has started a programme using radar satellites to track them, so that scientists can learn more about landslides and mudflows and try to predict them in future.

*These people are searching for survivors following a landslide in Peru in 1963, seven years before the terrible Mount Huascaran disaster.*

# LANDSLIDES & MUDFLOWS

**E**arthquakes often set off landslides, especially on steep mountains and coastal cliffs, which engulf everything in their paths. Where there is sandy soil or clay, the slightest vibration can bring down a whole slope. In 1920, an earthquake in central China started a large slide of loose soil that killed 200,000 people. Large rockfalls can be catastrophic, too. A magnitude 7.8 earthquake off the coast of Peru in 1970 started a landslide and avalanche of glacier ice on Mount Huascaran, the highest peak in the Peruvian Andes, and buried a whole town. Heavy rain can also cause rocks and soil loosened by earthquakes to flow downhill, and we call this a mudflow.

## RESCUE SERVICES

In the Andes mountains and elsewhere one of the great problems facing the rescue services is how to reach people who need help quickly. Landslides and mudflows wreck roads and railway lines. Helicopters are the most effective means of rescue. Even if they cannot land, they can winch people up from the ground, or lower or drop medical and food supplies.

# MAN-MADE QUAKES

**E**arthquakes are caused by natural forces. But it is possible that humans can cause quakes, or at least make them more likely, by greatly affecting the outer layer of the Earth's surface. Nuclear explosions used to be frequently carried out under desert regions, giving out tremendous energy and acting like earthquakes. Putting water into the ground can also cause tremors. This was discovered when waste water from a factory was pumped into boreholes under the ground near Denver, Colorado, in the USA. It was stopped when scientists realized that earth tremors increased as more water was pumped in. Many dam projects have also been blamed for earthquakes, as the water in reservoirs weighs down on the ground below and seeps into cracks and faults.

### CONTROLLING THE NILE

Before the Aswan High Dam was built to hold back the waters of the Nile, the temple of Ramses II at Abu Simbel in Egypt, built over 3,000 years ago, was cut into blocks and moved to **higher ground to save it from flooding.** The Aswan Dam was opened in 1971, creating Lake Nasser, a reservoir more than 500 km (311 miles) long. There were no records of any large earthquakes in the area, but in 1981, a magnitude-5.6 quake struck the lake. The epicentre was about 60 km (37 miles) upstream from the Dam, under the bed of the lake.

### HOOVER DAM

The Hoover Dam holds back the waters of the Colorado River at the end of the Grand Canyon, on the Arizona–Nevada border, **USA.** When the dam was completed in 1936, it created an enormous reservoir, called Lake Mead. As the reservoir filled up, tremors were felt in the region. When it was almost full, a magnitude-5 earthquake rattled the city of Las Vegas, 40 km (25 miles) away. Fortunately no damage was done to the dam, and the tremors died away. Today, the Hoover Dam supplies water and hydroelectric power over a wide area.

*In 1997, villagers near a new reservoir in Lesotho, in southern Africa, fled when a crack 1.5 km (1 mile) long and 7 cm (3 inches) wide opened up. Since the Katse reservoir began to fill in 1995, people in the Lesotho highlands have felt many small tremors.*

## LAKE KARIBA

**The Kariba Dam, across the Zambezi River on the Zambia/Zimbabwe border in southern Africa, made a lake eight times bigger than the lake created by the Hoover Dam.** As Lake Kariba was filling up between 1958 and 1961, the region was shaken by more than 2,000 tremors. The biggest was magnitude 5.8. The tremors stopped once the reservoir was full.

*Parts of the region around Lake Kariba have been made into a nature reserve.*

## WATER PRESSURE

**We now know that underground water can cause pressure to build up and rocks to slip.** At Rangely, in Colorado, scientists tried a controlled experiment by pumping water at high pressure into existing deep oil wells. They measured the amount of water absorbed by the underground rocks and used seismographs to check for tremors. They found that the higher the water pressure, the more small tremors were recorded. It appeared that the water lubricated faults in the rocks, causing them to slip and shake the ground.

# MEXICO CITY, 1985

**T**he western coast of Mexico forms part of the 'Ring of Fire' that surrounds the Pacific Ocean. Here the Cocos Plate beneath the ocean slides slowly under the lighter North American Plate, forming a deep underwater trench. At 7.18 on the morning of 19 September 1985, rocks slipped along a 200-km (124-mile) fault in this region, moving a distance of 2 metres (7 ft) in two separate jerks, 26 seconds apart. The focus of the earthquake was 20 km (12 miles) below the surface, near the coast of the Mexican state of Michoacan. The quake released as much energy as a thousand Hiroshima bombs and measured 8.1 on the Richter scale. One minute later, the seismic waves reached Mexico City, 380 km (236 miles) away, rolling in at 24,139 km/h (15,000 mph). Within five minutes, more than 400 buildings in the city collapsed and a further 3,000 were badly damaged. Official figures listed 9,500 people dead, but the exact figure may never be known.

### AZTEC CAPITAL

According to legend, the Aztecs were told to settle where they found a special sign – an eagle on a cactus grasping a snake. In about 1325 they found it, on a marshy island in Lake Texcoco, and built their capital, Tenochtitlan, there. The Aztec capital was destroyed by Spanish conquerors in 1521, and Mexico City was built in its place. When the earthquake struck in 1985, the vibrations in the old lake bed intensified, rattling the buildings in the city above.

### MONITORING THE QUAKE

At the U.S. National Earthquake Information Centre in Golden, Colorado, alarms were set off at 7.23, four minutes after Mexico City shook. Surface waves were monitored as arriving at the Centre, about 2,500 km (1,553 miles) from the epicentre, another five minutes later. The Centre issues reports on earthquakes throughout the world, and has located more than a quarter of a million quakes since it opened in 1973.

## MEXICO CITY

*A family who lived on the ground floor of a 14-floor apartment block believe they were saved by their pet parrot. The building collapsed on top of them and the parrot started screaming. Rescuers heard the screams and managed to reach the buried family eight hours later.*

*The Aztec capital of Tenochtitlan was a city of islands connected by canals. The waterways and gardens of Xochimilco, to the south of present-day Mexico City, are all that is left of the canals.*

## SEARCHING THE WRECKAGE

**Rescue workers were able to pull many survivors from the wreckage of collapsed apartment buildings. More than 30,000 people were injured, and at least 100,000 were made homeless.** Survivors can sometimes be trapped for days in collapsed buildings. Rescuers have the difficult task of locating survivors and then moving rubble safely. Specially-trained dogs and infrared or heat-sensitive equipment are used to help rescuers find people. In poorer regions of the world, where such equipment is not available, the rescue services have a much more difficult job.

## CLEANING UP

**In 1985, Mexico City had a total population of about 18 million. Most of the city's people were affected in some way by the earthquake.** Many of the homeless were put up in tents until new accommodation could be found. At first they simply had to look after themselves. Disease can easily spread after any natural disaster, if there is a lack of clean water and healthy food. Some of the collapsed buildings were hospitals, and rescuers searching for survivors found a total of 58 newborn babies beneath the ruins. Some had been buried for up to seven days. It is thought they survived because their bodies behaved as though they were still in the womb.

# HONSHU, JAPAN

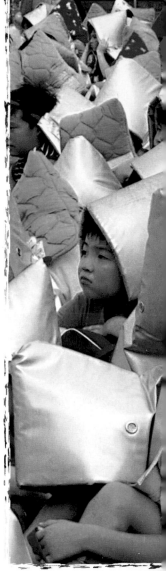

**TOKYO, 1923**

**These survivors searched among the rubble for their lost possessions.** Two huge fires had broken out in the city from overturned stoves, setting the wooden houses alight. Fires caused most of the casualties. At the same time some areas around the city were lifted up by 2 metres (7 ft), and the floor of Tokyo Bay moved 3 metres (10 ft) northwards. The nearby city of Yokohama was also badly hit, and the *London Times* correspondent reported that Yokohama had been 'wiped off the map'.

**J**apan is situated where four of the Earth's plates meet – the Eurasian and North American Plates to the north, and the Philippine and Pacific Plates to the south. So it is not surprising that the islands have many volcanoes and suffer 1,000 earthquakes every year. Most of the earthquakes are quite mild, but in 1923, a magnitude-8.3 quake shook a huge area of Honshu, Japan's largest island, including Japan's capital city, Tokyo. Over half a million houses were reduced to rubble, and 143,000 people died, 100,000 in Tokyo alone. Then, in 1995, the very south of the island, about 440 km from Tokyo, was hit. The industrial port of Kobe suffered the worst damage with collapsing buildings and ruptured gas mains bursting into flames all over the city. Many of the city's newer buildings survived, however, because they had been built with earthquakes in mind.

**KOBE, 1995**

**The quake that struck at 5.46 on the morning of 17 January 1995 measured 7.2 on the Richter scale.** The city of Kobe shook for 20 seconds, and the concrete pillars holding up a 600-metre (1,968-ft) section of the Hanshin Expressway linking Kobe with Osaka collapsed. The elevated expressway toppled and crashed. In all, 5,500 people were killed by the earthquake.

**LIVING WITH QUAKES**

Japanese children learn earthquake drills as a matter of course, including familiarizing themselves with special flameproof and waterproof headgear. In Tokyo, 1 September is known as Disaster Prevention Day. On the anniversary of the terrible Tokyo quake, remembrance services are held for victims.

**NAMAZU**

**According to ancient Japanese legend, earthquakes are caused by the namazu, a giant catfish living in mud.** In 1855 an earthquake struck Tokyo, which was then called Edo, and people believed that the namazu had been hurling itself around. It is said that before the 1923 quake catfish were seen jumping in ponds. In recent years, proper scientific studies have been made to see if catfish could be useful in predicting earthquakes, but without any great success.

## EVACUEES

**The Kobe earthquake destroyed 100,000 houses, and a further 88,000 were badly damaged.** More than 300,000 people were evacuated from their homes, and many lived in refugee camps for many weeks; 70,000 people were still living in shelters two months later. During this period there were thousands of small aftershocks, which made many believe that another major earthquake was on its way. Fortunately, this didn't happen.

The Kobe quake broke the city's water mains. About a million homes were without water for 10 days, so people had to queue for small supplies. Gas and electricity were also shut off, and 2 million homes were left without power.

## TOKYO & KOBE

It was discovered that a 90-year-old woman rescued from her home after the Kobe earthquake had also been a victim of the Tokyo quake 72 years earlier. In 1923, she was working in an office in Yokohama, and hid under a desk to avoid being crushed as the building collapsed. She moved some years later when her husband was transferred by his company from Yokohama to Kobe.

## POSEIDON

**In Greek mythology, Poseidon was the god of earthquakes and later of the sea.** He is sometimes known as the 'earth-shaker'. Poseidon was the brother of Zeus, and is usually portrayed as a supremely powerful god who was involved in many battles. The Greeks saw him as representing the violent forces of nature, and they sacrificed bulls in his honour.

# UNCOVERING THE PAST

**E**arthquakes have been happening for millions of years. In ancient times, it was thought that all natural disasters were brought about by the gods. Earthquakes, along with thunder and lightning, floods and droughts, were seen as signs that the gods were angry. Three of the Seven Wonders of the Ancient World – the Mausoleum, Colossus and Pharos – were shaken to the ground by quakes. The first great palace at Knossos, built by the Minoans, had already suffered this fate around 1700 BC. The citizens of the Roman cities of Pompeii and Herculaneum felt very strong tremors and suffered damage in AD 63, 16 years before Mount Vesuvius erupted and destroyed both. But at that time little or nothing was known about the links between earthquakes and volcanoes.

## THE FIRST MAUSOLEUM

**Mausolus was ruler of Caria, part of the Persian Empire.** He planned a huge tomb, the Mausoleum, for himself and his Queen, Artemisia, which was completed shortly after his death in 353 BC. In the 13th century AD, the Mausoleum was knocked down by an earthquake. Hundreds of years later statues and sculptures, such as these which archaeologists believe show the king and queen, were excavated at the site in modern-day Turkey.

*The Pharos lighthouse was built in the 3rd century BC to guide ships safely into the harbour of Alexandria, in Egypt. This was probably the world's first lighthouse. At the top was a fire, and sheets of bronze reflected its light out to sea. In 1324, the Pharos was destroyed by an earthquake, and some years later Muslims used the ruins to build a military fort.*

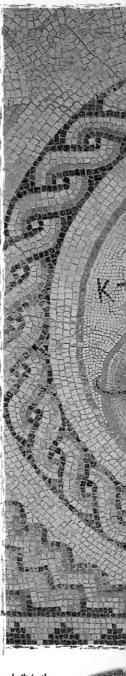

## KOURION, CYPRUS

**On 21 July 365, a great earthquake struck the eastern Mediterranean region.** Scientists believe that its epicentre was on the sea floor, about 50 km (31 miles) off the coast of Cyprus. The quake killed thousands on the island, and at the coastal town of Kourion archaeologists have discovered skeletons, pots, vases and many other artefacts, such as this mosaic, beneath the ruins.

## TEMPLE OF ZEUS

**The ancient Greeks worshipped Zeus, king of the gods, at Olympia.** An enormous statue of Zeus, made of ivory, gold and precious stones, stood in its own temple and became one of the Wonders of the World. The statue was shipped to Constantinople in AD 462, and about 100 years later, the whole region of Olympus was shaken by earthquakes. The temple and stadium were destroyed by landslides and floods, and were only excavated in recent times. Just a few columns (above) remain today.

*Today, bronze deer stand on pillars at each side of the entrance of Mandraki harbour, where Colossus once stood.*

## A FALLEN STATUE

**Mandraki harbour, on the Greek island of Rhodes, was believed to be protected by a giant bronze statue of Helios, the sun god.** The statue, called the Colossus, had one foot on either side of the harbour, but in about 226 BC, it was toppled by an earthquake and snapped off at the knees. The people of Rhodes were told by an oracle not to rebuild the statue, so they left it lying where it fell.

## LASER TECHNOLOGY

**In California, lasers are used to measure the tiniest ground movements with total accuracy.** Laser beams are sent out from this station and aimed at reflectors on the other side of known fault lines. Sensitive instruments measure the time it takes beams to reach the reflector and back, so that any tiny change in distance caused by ground movement is detected. This is a very accurate system that can be constantly monitored.

## HAICHENG

**Early in 1975, seismologists noticed that water levels in wells around the city of Haicheng, in northeast China, were changing.** Then small tremors started. Around a million people were evacuated from their homes in the region on the morning of 4 February, and that evening a magnitude-7.5 quake devastated the region. Thousands of buildings collapsed and 1,328 people were killed. Without the warning, it would have been many thousands more.

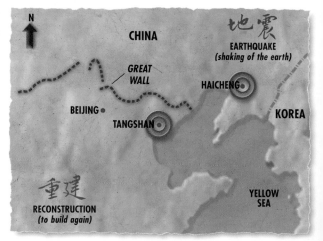

N

CHINA

地震
EARTHQUAKE
(shaking of the earth)

GREAT
WALL

HAICHENG

BEIJING

TANGSHAN

KOREA

重建
RECONSTRUCTION
(to build again)

YELLOW
SEA

## CHECKING GROUNDWATER

*Scientists have found that the amounts of minerals and gases present in groundwater can change before an earthquake, as rocks move and the water is squeezed from one crack to another, so water levels are checked regularly.*

## TANGSHAN

**Less than 18 months after the Haicheng quake, a much greater disaster struck the city of Tangshan, 400 km (249 miles) away.** This time there was no forecast and no warning. The epicentre of a magnitude-7.9 earthquake was right in the city, with catastrophic results. The official death toll was 242,000, but it is possible that more than half a million people died.

# PREDICTING EARTHQUAKES

**S**eismologists are constantly looking for new methods that will help them to forecast when and where major earthquakes will occur. Some scientists believe that strong earthquakes are less likely to happen in areas where weak quakes are common, because the small tremors relieve the stress that otherwise would lead to a major jolt. In high-risk areas in the USA and Japan, experiments are being conducted to detect the tiniest movements along fault lines. Scientists hope that this will help them predict a possible larger movement in the future, so that people can be evacuated from danger zones. They have also found that changes in the level and content of underground water can tell us a lot about the movement and possible cracking of rocks.

### CREEPMETERS

**Creepmeters, which measure the creep, or movement, of a fault can be used to detect minute changes.** Scientists believe that the more data they can acquire about small ground movements over many years, the easier it will become to recognize changes in the normal pattern. These changes may show that a big quake is on its way.

## PARKFIELD, CALIFORNIA

**Parkfield lies on the San Andreas Fault, almost exactly halfway between San Francisco and Los Angeles.**
It is the most intensely monitored section of any earthquake zone in the world.
The arrows show the direction in which the fault is slowly sliding.

**1** An underground seismometer measures the smallest tremor.

**2** A magnetometer measures changes in the Earth's magnetic field, which tell scientists about stress on underground rocks.

**3** A seismometer near the surface records larger tremors.

**4** A vibrating instrument creates shock waves to probe the earthquake zone.

**5** A creepmeter measures ground movement at the surface very precisely.

**6** A strainmeter measures any underground deformation of rock produced by strain, and transmits this to a satellite.

**7** A sensor constantly checks groundwater level; the results are also sent to the satellite.

**8** A space satellite receives data from Parkfield and beams the information to a main geological survey station.

**9** Lasers measure any ground movement across the fault by bouncing beams off reflectors **10**.

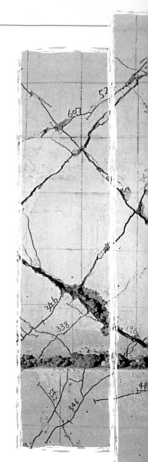

# LOOKING TO THE FUTURE

**S**cientists have tried to find ways of reducing the strength of earthquakes, for example by pumping water under ground to lubricate faults and allow rocks to slide past each other with less shock and more warning. So far these experiments have not been very successful, and we will probably never be able to stop earthquakes. However, we can try to learn much more about them, so that more precautions and warnings can be given, saving lives and also saving cities and towns from total destruction. Buildings can be constructed with earthquakes in mind, and modern technology can be used to forecast where and when disasters are likely to happen.

## SHOCK ABSORBERS

**Rubber and steel pads, called isolators, can be put under new or existing buildings to make them more earthquake-resistant – just like this exhibit in a California museum.** The isolators act as shock absorbers, and the space around them lets the building shake without collapsing. Tall buildings must be able to sway without cracking, just as they do in high winds. To make them safer, walls are made of reinforced concrete and are strengthened with steel beams.

## LEARNING MORE

**The more we learn about earthquakes, the better we will be able to survive them.** There are banks of seismographs and other equipment at the US Geological Survey's laboratories in Menlo Park, California. Seismologists all over the world share information, about past earthquakes and possible future ones. They also use computer programmes to see what might happen in particular areas if an earthquake were to strike.

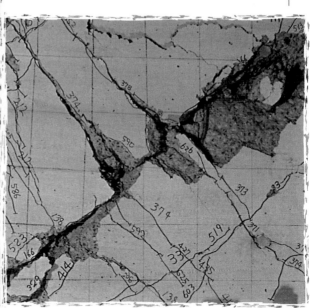

## LEADERS IN EARTHQUAKE RESEARCH

**The forces of nature reveal their secrets to a Japanese scientist, among the world leaders in seismological research.**
The Building Research Institute in Tsukuba has the world's largest earthquake study facility. Architects and engineers use vibrating machines to test models of new buildings, producing the same effect as an earthquake and regulated to different magnitudes. The models are tested to destruction, to learn how much vibration they can withstand. Technicians map every crack after these simulated tremors.

## SURVIVAL KIT

*In earthquake zones, many homes and offices are equipped with survival kits. Their equipment and supplies can help people stay alive if they are trapped for a long time.*

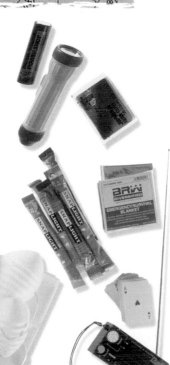

*This pyramid-shaped 48-floor skyscraper is San Francisco's tallest building, at 260m (853 ft) high. Its shape was specially designed to withstand earthquakes. It was completed in 1972 and is used as an office block.*

# DID YOU KNOW?

Around the world, more than 1.5 million people have died in earthquakes in this century.

The longest earthquake ever recorded rumbled on for four minutes – in Alaska, in 1964.

Light flashes might warn us of earthquakes. Some survivors say they saw flashes of red and blue light shortly before the Kobe earthquake struck in 1995. Scientists think this effect might have been caused by a phenomenon called fractoluminescence. This happens when a mineral found in many rocks, called quartz, is fractured.

Prisoners have escaped from jail during many of the world's major earthquakes. One escapee was Captain Greaves, a famous pirate who was known to never rob the poor or mistreat any of his own prisoners. Greaves was imprisoned for piracy in 1680, but escaped when an earthquake destroyed the prison. He later won a pardon.

Earthquake-proof buildings were built as early as 1904. The American architect and engineer, Julia Morgan (1872-1957), built a bell-tower of reinforced concrete in San Francisco in 1904. There were very few woman architects in those days, and this choice of materials was considered very unusual. But when the structure withstood the terrible 1906 earthquake, Morgan's reputation was made.

Earthquakes have helped us learn about our human ancestors. Olduvai Gorge, an archaeological site on the Serengeti Plains in northern Tanzania, has provided scientists with unique evidence for early human evolution from millions of years ago. A prehistoric earthquake cut through the plains and formed the jagged rift of the gorge, exposing the shores of a dried-up lake to view. Many remains of early humanlike creatures have been found in the region.

During the first moon landing in 1969, astronauts Neil Armstrong and Buzz Aldrin set up scientific instruments on the moon, including a seismometer. Before long the first evidence of a 'moonquake' had been sent back to Earth.

It may seem that there are more earthquakes every year, but according to records this is not the case. There is because of the increase in the number of seismographic stations in the world.

## ACKNOWLEDGEMENTS

We would like to thank: Graham Rich, Hazel Poole and Elizabeth Wiggans for their assistance. Artwork by Peter Bull Art Studio.
Copyright © 1999 ticktock Publishing Ltd.
First published in Great Britain by ticktock Publishing Ltd., The Offices in the Square, Hadlow, Tonbridge, Kent TN11 0DD, Great Britain.
All rights reserved.
No part of this publication may be reproduced, stored in a retrieval system, or transmitted in any form or by any means electronic, mechanical, photocopying, recording or otherwise, without prior written permission of the copyright owner.
A CIP catalogue record for this book is available from the British Library. ISBN 1 86007 107 4 (paperback). ISBN 1 86007 120 1 (hardback).

Picture research by Image Select. Printed in Hong Kong.

Picture Credits: t = top, b = bottom, c = centre, l = left, r= right, OFC = outside front cover, OBC = outside back cover, IFC = inside front cover

Ancient Art & Architecture; 26bl, 27tr. Colorific; 8/9 (main pic) & OFC, 14tl, 26/27 (main pic). Corbis; 6tl, 12tl, 12/13 (main pic), 18c, 21b, 22tl, 22/23t, 23br, 24tl, 31br, 31tl, 30/31b. Image Select; 12bl, 14br, 17br, 20bl, 20tl, 26tl, 26/27cb. Mary Evans; 15br. National Geographic Society; 16br, 18/19br & OBC, 19tr, 22b, 23cr, 30/31 (main pic) & 32. Oxford Scientific Films; 2bc, 2/3 (main pic), 5tr, 5cl, 6/7 (main pic), 16tl. Planet Earth Pictures; 4/5 (main pic), 20/21 (main pic), 24b. Popperfoto; 24/25 (main pic) & IFC, 8br, 24cl, 24/25 (main pic). Rex; 5bc, 25cl, 27br. Science & Society; 13tr. Science Photo Library; 2bl, 4tl, 6cb, 8bl, 10/11 (main pic), 14/15 (main pic), 14/15c, 16/17 (main pic), 28/29 (main pic), 28bl, 29tr, 29br, 30bl. Telegraph Colour Library; 10/11cb. Tony Stone Images; OFC (inset pic), 5cr, 8tl & OBC.

Every effort has been made to trace the copyright holders and we apologize in advance for any unintentional omissions.
We would be pleased to insert the appropriate acknowledgement in any subsequent edition of this publication.